Y0-CKL-418

COLLECTED POEMS OF MARY WHITE SLATER

By Mary White Slater
_____

The Child Book
Collected Poems

MARY WHITE SLATER

MARY WHITE SLATER

Collected Poems

EXPOSITION PRESS · NEW YORK

FIRST EDITION

All rights reserved including the right of reproduction in whole or in part in any form
Copyright, 1953, by Mary White Slater
Published by the Exposition Press Inc.
386 Fourth Avenue, New York 16, N.Y.
Designed by Morry M. Gropper
Manufactured in the United States of America
Consolidated Book Producers, Inc.
Library of Congress catalog card number: 52-13050

To Peggy, with my love

Acknowledgments

Acknowledgments for permission to reprint previously published poems are made—

To *Harper's Magazine* for the use of "The Pool"
To Harriet Monroe's *Poetry* for the use of "Barefoot Sandals"
To the *Cosmopolitan* for the use of "The First Day at School," "The Live Doll," and "The Sandman"
To the *Delineator* and *The Designer* for the use of other delineations of children in verse
To the *Radio–TV Mirror* for "I Flung a Rose to You" and "Butterfly"
To Dorrance & Co., Inc., for fifty-three poems from *The Child Book*
To the New York *Herald-Tribune* for the use of "Huntsman" and "October"
To *Vistas*, and *Talaria*, and to *The Forum Magazine* for the use of "The Murderer"

The author wishes to express her profound gratitude to Mercedes Canfield Hunter and Margaret Moak Shoffstall, for their help in getting this book ready for publication.

Contents

Poetry: An Essay by a Lay Poet	11

I

A Study of History	23
Interplay	24
At the Lecture	25
Elan Vital	26
Huntsman	27
At Oberammergau	28
New Year's Eve	29
We Are the Gods	30
"God"	31
Credo	32
Once on a Greening Planet	33
Hertha	34
The Atom Speaks	35
Man	36
We Live by Faith	37
The Things We Live By	38
I Have Loved Beauty	39
Beauty—Beauty—	40
If I Can Rescue	41

II

James William Slater	43
Twilight After Rain	45
A Whiff of Lilacs	46

III

Ballerina	47
Butterfly	48
My Sycamore	48
October	49
The Pool	50

Indian Summer	51
Event	51
Saint Joseph's	53
Barefoot Sandals	54
Brenda Passes	55
Lilacs	56
When Spring Comes Down to Shottery	57
At Easter	58
Nirvana	58
Resurrection	59
The Mother	60
Through a Cool Green Gateway	61
Shiela	62
The Easter Child	63
Oh, For a Ship	64
The Prince of the Ragged School	65
The Guest	66
Blind Girl	67
Burbank	68
Father Cotter	69
John Campbell	70
Old Aleck	72
When Lisa Sang at Carnegie	73
Baby Nancy	74
When Her Ship Comes In	75
Autumn Leaves	76
Dogwood	77
What the Summer Said	78
Snowing	79
November	80
Plum Tree	81
Rose	82
Robin	83
Bee	84
Dandelion	85
Winter River	86
April Snow	87
September	88

The Flying Fish	89
Sea Shell	90
Pasadena	91
Broadway	92
The Goldfish	93
Motoring	94
The Wind	95
The Tree	96

IV

When Father Cotter Rings the Bells	97
The Elm Tree	98
The Great House in the Square	99
To a Child	100
The Venturer	100
The First Day of School	101
The Scholar	102
You'd Better Eat Your Dinner	103
On Mother's Wedding Day	104
As Janet Dances	105
The Lake	106
The Sandman	107
That Bold Baby Donna	108
At the Font	109
I Wonder	110
Rain	111
Measles	112
The Locomotive	113
On the Stoop	114
The Live Doll	115
The Wanderer	116
I Made Some Hills Against a Sky	117
I'm Making Me an Airship	118
Bed Time	118
Grandfather's House	119
On Hallowe'en	120
The Ghost	121
The Roller Skater	122

All Day Across the River	123
The Man in the Moon	124
Promoted	125
Last Night	127
At the Window	128
Our Flag	129
The Exile	130
The Swimmers	131
Nap Time	133
Once—	134

V

I Must Have Thirsted	135
A Look—A Light	136
I Burn a Secret Candle	137
I Flung a Rose	138
Sometimes in Dreams	139
Jealousy	140
You Are So Cold	141
White Blooms	141
Believe in Me	142
Like a Comet	143
Your Silence Is Like God's	143
All Cool and Blue	144
Fiesole	145

VI

Europe—1914	147
Noël	148
Christmas Wine—1940	149
May Was Not May—1917	150
Target—Berlin, 1918	151
Christmas 1939	152
Hitler	153
America, 1942	153
Children Evacuated From London, 1943	154
Gandhi	155
The Murderer (1915)	156

POETRY *An Essay by a Lay Poet*

The poet deals with life—and life is the supreme mystery. We are all born poets. We know it by being lives—by experiencing life. It is our ultimate reality. A true poet is known by his acute sense of life and by a creative passion to embody in words life's rhythms, harmonies and dissonances.

The word "life" used to connote plants, animals and men. It has now come to connote a living universe. The universe, which used to be a big thing made up of a number of things moving in a big space, is now conceived as an *event*, a creative process in action, a living form. Matter is found to be *motion*, the interaction of opposing forces, its solidity being only an appearance to the eye. Stars, plants, animals and humans are evidenced by appearance and disappearance. True time is the unbroken creative action of life itself, the fourth dimension—which includes our old conception of time and space. God is the mind-energy immanent in a *living universe*, and man, awakened to his evolutional rank in time, finds himself the highest creative ability and responsibility as yet evolved on this planet.

Twentieth-century physics, in finding *matter to be motion*, and the *universe an event*, forced man to make a new and transcendent click of consciousness.

Matter, the hitherto solid ground for his mental feet, dissolves into nothingness, lets him drop into the impalpable. He falls endlessly, gasping, suffocating, giddy, repudiating yet clutching for his solid plank, until eventually he finds himself whirling round the axis of his new ideas as unsustained by material support as the earth is in atmosphere. To sense matter as energy is necessary for the world view of the twentieth century. The mathematics of solids is augmented by the mathematics of motion. Our world view and our knowledge is shown to be relative to our place in the life flow, and the universe sensed as mind-energy in creative action shifts the idea of creation by evolution from the physical to the mental and spiritual. Einstein identifies mathematics as a *religious* science and states that our most important function is to rouse it and keep it alive.

Poets, prophets and seers have always intuited man's essential oneness with the creative process, and have always had an intimate sense of the rhythmic nature of life.

This planet swings round its sun on its own stem through the rhythmic quatrains of spring, summer, autumn and winter. Every life-form on this planet moves through the same measures of birth, growth, fruition and death. Even universes mark time to this remarkable beat of destiny—this couplet of life—appearance and disappearance. And man finds himself a highly sensitized part of this creative process. We know we are incarnations of an all-pervading force, and that the throb of our hearts is one with its first beat. We realize that out of the nebular came suns and planets, and that on this planet came plants, animals and humans—a crystal, a rose, a tiger, a cave man and a *Jesus*.

Looking backward, we can see that the reformer as well as the poet has always been of poetic fiber; both see life with a passionate concern for its direction. Say Buddha and Paul. Say Dante, Goethe, Shakespeare, Milton, Shelley, Emerson and Whitman. Say Nietzsche, Omar and Job. Say Hitler and the communists in our time, and you have named spirits—rebels all—who have evidenced life in creative action—with its rhythms, its harmonies or its dissonances.

Some children are cosmic in their attitude toward the world, and are naturally poets.

While all men are poets in some degree, not all are artists. The actual poet is an artist dealing with words as expressions of realities. And an artist, whether his name is Shakespeare, Praxiteles, Michaelangelo, Wagner, Thomas Jefferson or John L. Lewis, *experiences* beauty and truth by creative energies in action.

The really creative artist uses form and content as *means* and never as ends in themselves. The creative mind is one for all time, but it comes in contact with ever-changing conditions. As the form which once served as a vehicle for spiritual energy gradually undergoes imitation, or becomes an end in itself, the artist is compelled to repudiate the form for a new vehicle.

We have all seen how certainly life rises, in the long run, to repudiate any form, whether of religious creed, art, governmental or industrial system, that holds it to less than it ought to be. In fact, as we look back on the long martyrdom of man, we see registered in the governmental forms, at the price of much blood and many tears, the rise of the spirit of man toward more and more creative freedom for action—or toward democracy. The cry is always, Government is for man, not man for government. In 1914 we saw the whole world rise against a governmental idea of life for the survival of the physically fit. By 1918 we had paid the price of many millions of lives and billions of dollars for the idea that life is for the survival of the spiritually fit. The Second World War was an even more costly event—even more directly a conflict between these two opposing philosophical tenets. And the costs mount higher and the battle continues in the "cold war" of today.

We are seeing the same thing in the industrial world—the rise of life itself against a system that makes man subservient to the machine. The cry of labor is that the machine is for man, and not man for the machine. And what price we shall have to pay in blood, tears and dollars before the proper adjustment comes is for our immediate future to answer.

We are seeing in religion the revolt of the spirit against outgrown creeds that do not square with the facts and findings of life —the struggle of the Calvinistic idea of a mechanical universe, against the present idea of a universe of energy and change. Here again life is crying, creeds are for man, not man for creeds.

So in the world of music we are seeing the revolt of life, the creative spirit, against the imperialism of old forms. Modern composers are crying, Music is for life, not life for music. So we have the revolt of Wagner, Tschaikowski, Debussy, down to the radicalism of Shostakovich and the hoodlumism of "jazz" and "swing." It is part of the struggle of the creative spirit to break the forms that enclose it, the eternal struggle of life for more and more creative freedom.

So in painting and sculpture—revolting from the static expressions of beauty as untrue to life—the artist endeavors to embody the evolving consciousness that is man, the flow of life itself, whether on canvas, in marble, or in the "mobile." Here again life is crying, The artistic expression is for man—not man for the artistic expression.

In poetry the revolt is sometimes revolting when it goes as far as Gertrude Stein, but even here life reiterates its eternal cry.

The poet deals with language.
His passion is to express life in words that fit.
A word is a strictly human affair.

Only man on this planet has achieved articulate expression. To be man is to be articulate.

Few of us consider the miracle of language as an evolutional achievement. It shows the attempt to express emotion and thought by means of the articulation of air in the human throat. A word is an incarnation, a thought-form. It must have marked a definite reach in the creative process. It did mark the origin of a newly conscious species, a *leap* from *animal* to *man*. Think of the evolutionary struggle from the groping ejaculations of the cave man to the lyric ease of Burns.

The sentence must have taken centuries of approach. It achieves subject, predicate and object, and so tells a tale—the first short story. Then came the rich colorings and relational values of adjectives, adverbs, prepositions, moods and tenses, until language incarnates the inner events of man's mind and heart and brings men into greater understandings of themselves.

The essay shows man thinking himself into words.

The novel shows man imagining, dreaming, creating a world by words.

The lyric shows man singing dreams and emotions into words.

First poets knew no technique. They simply sang or chanted according to their moods.

In time poetry grew to be a fine art. A poem became a piece of verbal architecture involving the conquering of its word-material. As an artistic development of form, it took on techniques, described in the classroom by long-tailed words that can put a blight forever on the student's attitude toward poetry.

While it is true that a poet must not only be born, but made, equipped with the technical knowledge of his art, a poem is not a thing willed into being, by assemblage of parts, like a house or a car—verse may be that. A poem *grows* in the subsoil of the mind, is conceived there by the passionate coming together of thought and emotion in the pregnant dark of the soul. The short lyric, the purest form of poetry, sings itself out of an ecstasy, an orgasm of creative joy. The true poet is never primarily concerned with technique or form. His thought and emotion determine the form. His verbal response to life comes in the pulse and rhythm of his own nature. Every poet, every man, has his own pulse, rhythm and ring.

There is a radical and eternal difference between verse and poetry. Verse may be merely a mechanical goose step of meter and rhyme *ad nauseam*—a mechanical means, a frame for advertising the writer's sentiments or philosophy of life, as is evidenced in most of the so-called poems read to us on the radio. In poetry it's imitate and be damned, for none but the poet achieves in words the breath of the rose or the powder on the butterfly. Even he is mostly in despair at the limitations of words as tools to depict the impalpable mystery of life.

There are rare uses of words that affect us electrically—with a shock of surprise and delight. They shoot into the brain with a uniqueness that makes the heart stop and the skin creep. Certain nuances of language bring intoxicating air from new distances, flooding the soul with a nostalgia unutterable. There are poems that make one rise into higher dimensions of consciousness. William James speaks of single words—passages of poems read to one in childhood—as "irrational doorways into the wildness, pang and mystery of life," and says that we are dead or alive in accordance with whether we have kept or lost this mystic sensibility.

A familiar expression of cosmic consciousness comes through the young Wordsworth's lines:

>   And I have felt
> A presence that disturbs me with the joy
> Of elevated thoughts. A sense sublime
> Whose dwelling is the light of setting suns,
> And the round ocean, and the living air,
> And the blue sky, and the mind of man.
> A motion and a spirit that impels
> All thinking things, all objects of thought,
> And rolls in all things.

Blake chants it in

> Tiger, tiger, burning bright
> In the forest of the night,
> What immortal hand or eye
> Could frame thy fearful symmetry?

Emerson awakens us to new insights in

> Count as many as you pass,
> Trefoils and violets in the grass,
> So many saints and saviors,
> So many high behaviors.

Francis Thompson gives his reaction in

> I fled Him, down the nights and down the days;
> I fled Him, down the arches of the years;

> I fled Him, down the labyrinthine ways
>   Of my own mind; and in the midst of tears
> I hid from Him, and under running laughter,
>   Up vistaed hopes, I sped;
>   And shot, precipitated,
> Adown Titanic glooms of chasmèd fears,
>   From those strong Feet that followed after.

Think of Omar's immortal quatrain on the Spirit of Life—

> Whose secret Presence through Creation's veins
> Running Quicksilver-like eludes your pains;
>   Taking all shapes from Máh to Máhi and
> They change and perish all—but He remains.

Hear Swinburne voicing the Universal Spirit—of which man is part—

> O my sons, O too dutiful
> *Toward gods not of me,*
> Was I not enough beautiful?
> Was it hard to be free?
> For behold, *I am with you, am in you and of you;*
>   Look forth now and see.
>
> One birth of my bosom;
> One beam of mine eye;
> One topmost blossom
> That scales the sky;
> *Man*, equal and one with me, man that is made of me,
>   *Man that is I.*

Oriental philosophy calls the Spirit of Life Cosmic Consciousness.

Science calls it Evolution.

Emerson calls it the Oversoul.

Maeterlinck calls it the Unknown Guest.

Bergson calls it the Elan Vital or Vital Impetus—which has forced its way up through life from chlorophyllian consciousness, animal instinct, and the intellect of man—which thinks "about it and about"—to the Intuition of Reality which reaches its high flowering in the poet and seer.

Most people call it Religion.

Jesus calls it the Holy Ghost.

Faith and doubt are opposing electrical poles that keep the human mind in creative action. The very mark of a growing mind is a faith that doubts, suspends judgment, searches, finds, discards all conclusions that do not square to increasing knowledge and experience.

The Book of Job is an imperishable poetic expression of man bombarded with adversities by God Himself. Out of it comes the cry:

> I know that my Redeemer liveth. . . .
> Though He slay me, yet will I trust Him.

And in contrast comes the chiding despair of Omar at a God not good enough to be true:

> Oh Thou, who Man of baser Earth didst make,
> And ev'n with Paradise devise the Snake;
>   For all the Sin wherewith the Face of Man
> Is blacken'd—Man's forgiveness give—and take!

Could there be a more arresting and confounding expression of baffled faith? Is this not a religious response of profound kind, involving bravery equal to—if opposite from—Job's? Man risen from his knees to his feet before the *Unknown*, with his head up —not down!

Not only the poet, and the intellectual elite, but great numbers of people today are injected with the new vistas of reality, into which science is constantly widening the aperture. There is nothing so blinding as new light, and the masses loyal to inherited creeds are slow to listen to, much less accept and adjust to, new and disturbing ideas. We all know that life in the long run always rises to throw off all yokes that hamper its passion for creative freedom. Somehow the poet, with his Intuition of Reality—along with the prophet and seer—is the first to sense what religion and science, trailing slowly in their wake, finally adjust to, prove and accept.

We have seen in all the arts today man turning away from the static expressions of the past and endeavoring to embody in marble, paint, music and words the motion, discord, imperfection and indeterminateness of life. And from this have issued the monstrosities of modern art forms that confound the mind of today.

The mark of a poet, then, seems to be an acute sense of life and a passion to share his intuition of reality in words that fit. A poet never loses this cosmic sense. He lives in divine discontent at his limitations, his glimpses of *reality*. Yet he is always the seer, the prophet, the philosopher, the rebel, the revolutionary—confronted with a challenging and baffling universe.

MARY WHITE SLATER

COLLECTED POEMS OF MARY WHITE SLATER

I

A Study of History

What Master dared to dream and write
   the baffling manuscript of night
   in syllables of suns at play
   conceiving planets wet with May?

What Eros dared to dream and sing
   the earthy orgasms of spring
   conceiving in green garden closes
   a myriad monsters, skylarks, roses?

What Poet dared to dream and plan
   a creature unresolved as man—
   the wakened, wondering, thinking clod,
   a blunderer—conceiving God?

Interplay

Pray not for peace alone, lest man
   forego creative strife,
   the impassioned urge for freedom
   that sets the pulse of life.

Pray not for love alone, lest man
   forego the noble hate
   that guards the roads of freedom
   against the tides of fate.

Nor pray for light alone, lest man
   forego the artistry
   of moonlit midnight darkness,
   and beauty cease to be.

At the Lecture

He weighed a star—a mastodon
   in mythical Orion
   entered an atom, spied upon
   the antics of an ion;

   reported what he found and saw
   with logical precision,
   unfolded four-dimensional law
   to aid our eager vision.

       *   *   *

We wished his logic could divine
   the reason for a rose,
   or for the fateful rebel line
   of Eve's inquiring nose;

   or that his calculus could give
   the universal why
   of all the blundering lives we live
   and all the deaths we die.

Elan Vital

Behold the Spirit of Life
   aspiring
   struggling

   out of the fecund fog of nebulae
   into whirl and rush
   of suns and planets

   in throb of mineral
   triumph of crystal
   creep of grass
   rise of tree
   explosion of rose

   in cold finesse of fish
   warm flash of birds
   witless wisdom of bee
   ferocity of a myriad wild
   stolidity of cow
   blind loyalty of dog

   in sad-eyed ape
   unchallenged by the midnight sky

   in man,
   whose wonder grips the stars,
   who dreams, thinks, blunders,
   dares, digs, climbs
   and wills his way
   toward infinite understandings.

Huntsman

Little man, little man,
   where have you been?

Nearer and farther
   than ever were seen—

Digging and diving,
   soaring apace,

Conquering time,
   shriveling space.

I shattered an atom
   and shuddered to find

A power to destroy
   or deliver mankind—

In the lair of an atom
   where no man had trod

I looked upon Lucifer
   challenging God.

At Oberammergau

Jesus and Judas, each fulfilled his role
   in that predestined drama of the soul.

Jesus, the Son of God, assuming birth,
   dooming Himself to death to save the earth—
Judas, the earthling of the traitor kiss,
   unconscious of a fate he could not miss.

We wept when gentle Jesus, crucified,
   called chidingly on God before he died,
and with the thousands gathered there to see,
   we wept for Mary's matchless misery,

Yet wondered if that Judas on the tree,
   sending himself to death in agony,
with neither God nor man on whom to call,
   were not the deeper tragedy of all.

New Year's Eve

The tide is low,
   the year is dying,
   the earth rolls on
   for all our trying
   to conquer time,
   arrest its flying—
   to cage the singing
   lark of youth,
   to rest from life
   its hidden truth—

The old, old earth
   goes rolling on
   indifferent to
   the human pack
   of blundering gods
   upon her back.

We Are the Gods

We are the gods and devils
   of a sodden star—
   risen from lower levels
   of life to what we are.

Eons before the pages
   of day and night began,
   deep in the mothering ages
   throbbed a pulse toward man.

We are the lovers and haters
   blind to the plot and the play,
   builders, destroyers, creators,
   each with a song or a say—

Some of us seers and saviors
   urged into acts sublime,
   calling to other behaviors
   to waken, rise and climb.

"*God*"

One April dawn
  a fool awoke
  and to his window ran
  dazed by a dream—
  a dream that God
  would show Himself to man.

And there below
  his window case
  to meet his mad desire,
  he saw a cool
  green lilac bush
  burning a cool green fire.

Alas for him
  who cannot see
  God rising in
  a lilac tree.

Credo

I believe in the God in man
   and in gods the sons of men—

Some holy human ghosts
   in whom dawn passionate ideas
   of the love, justice and mercy
   in which life ought to be lived—

Creators
   newly aware of their own responsibility
   to life and living conditions on their planet,
   fired with new powers,
   drawing men with them
   to peaks of nobler views and actions—

Fearing not crucifixions,
   deaths, descents into hells
   for truth's sake—
   dying, rising,
   conceiving ideas of God and man
   good enough to be true—

Declaring a heaven of noble action,
   a hell of low behavior,
   feeling God in themselves
   and themselves gods.

Once on a Greening Planet

Once on a greening planet
   that rolled around a sun
   there lived a brainy people—
   my tale is almost done.

Upon their greening planet
   that turned from day to night
   they learned a secret of the stars,
   the sun, the atom's might.

Amid their singing steeples
   (to tell it is to weep)
   with gallant pleas to heaven
   before they fell asleep,

They built themselves a rocket
   (a sorry thing to say)
   that blew their greening planet
   and all their brains away.

Hertha

He must hold human blunderers dear
   to hang such beauty on the year,

     to make of earth a garden close
     for sunrise, sunset, robin, rose,

     with rivers pouring endlessly
     alluring pathways to the sea,

     to coin a moon and spin it high
     across a spangled deep of sky,

     to heap the hills that make us climb
     above the frets of space and time

     and etch upon our lifted sight
     an ordered majesty of night

     besetting star-enchanted eyes
     with challenges toward paradise.

His tide of beauty never fails us
   whatever fate arraigns, assails us,

     abiding beauty at life's core
     gives something to be thankful for.

The Atom Speaks

I am the apple of desire—
    in Eden my forbidden fire
    enamored Eve, closed heaven's gate,
    made death the seal of human fate.

Now that you've climbed the knowledge-tree,
    adventurous man, to savor me,
    take care lest what you hope to find
    betray instead of bless your kind,

And when you take your treasure-trove
    home—to the lips of those you love—
    beware lest my unfettered fire
    destroy all hope and all desire.

Man

We live by law. To seize its tools,
   to map the past and future by its rules,
   our highest freedom. Shall advancing man
   deny a Source as he divines a plan?—

A plan that rolls into the abyss of time
   unnumbered suns in pageantry sublime,
   that flings out worlds as gardeners scatter grain—
   and one all pregnant with the human pain;

A pain that wakens to a three-score sigh
   the creature man, with wistful wondering eye
   to love, work, blunder to his daily sleep
   and somehow find the law his soul shall keep;

To glimpse the grim immensity that hurled
   the throbbing seed that man has called his world,
   pulsing with fire and flood, with quake and shock,
   blooming with blessings, blessing oft to mock,

And yet to keep the faith, though worlds decline,
   in purpose somehow good, in thought divine,
   and in the mystery of his human soul
   discern a flower of some stupendous whole.

We Live by Faith

We live by faith, chafe as we may at creeds;
   we work the plough of law to fill our needs
   and sleep like children, though we toss and sigh
   as earth, our cradle, swings across the sky.

We read in every sunset's line of gold,
   sunrise shall come. The glorious fact is old,
   yet, like young children fearful of night's gloom,
   we wait the moon's pale rise, the stars' white bloom.

Whether we mock or pray or wondering scan,
   or dare to measure God and show his plan,
   behind our blunderings stand love and pain
   and our still faith in law's eternal reign.

Whoever waits upon tomorrow's sun
   trusts God unconsciously. And everyone
   who hopes gives hostage to the future's thrall,
   and by that hope declares his faith in all.

The Things We Live By

We live by beauty—though no song we sing,
   our nostrils know the ecstasy of spring,
   warm whiffs of rain on lilacs cold as snow—
   our eyes know hills at dawn and evening glow.

We live by love—though never our love we meet,
   home, comrades, children, work and play are sweet,
   books, firelight, dogs; a window to the moon
   and stars rose-white in midnight's black lagoon.

We live by faith—though never a prayer we say,
   we trust the earth to roll from night to day,
   the tides of grass to break in foaming flowers,
   the fountain trees to rise in cool green showers.

We live by hope—though loved and lovers die—
   that death brings wakening to another sky,
   and when our shining beads of day are said,
   like children we fall trustingly to bed.

I Have Loved Beauty

I have loved beauty. Say this then of me
   when I breathe out into the unknown sea
   that flows around the world. On that slight spar
   a mariner may reach the central star
   if beauty be a true divining rod
   to point a sailor to the heart of God.

Lord of all beauty, on the dusky stool
   of earth at twilight sits a singing fool—
   one of Your hungry, hapless human things
   born on the ground and passionate for wings—
   born of the dark and passionate for light,
   enchanted at the spangled deep of night,
   enraptured at a child, a dog, a rose,
   a stripling moon above earth's garden close,
   a river shimmering toward a sunset bar—
   the stabbing beauty of a lone white star,

A silent swimmer in a silent sea
   of unflawed purple, unaware of me,
   a human hunter eager as a youth
   after a grail—the shining cup of truth
   that lures and leads me like a lovely wraith
   delighting in my doubtings and my faith.

Lord of all beauty of this earth and sky,
   forever challenging the human eye,
   the ear to hear, the tongue to try to say
   what nostrils know in April and in May,
   fail not an answering heart, a questing mind—
   be faithful to a worshipper and kind.

Beauty—Beauty—

Beauty—Beauty whom I see
   through a prison glass
   inviting and evading me
   as up and down you pass—

When you waken, stretch and rise
   dewy, naked, sweet,
   morning-glories in your eyes
   and tangled in your feet—

When you come running, raining, blowing
   up the April hill,
   petal-cool and petals throwing
   at my window sill—

When you walk in twilight blue
   down the limpid west
   in a slender moonlit shoe
   with one star in your breast—

Beauty, Beauty, for the power
   to stop you on your way
   and hold you for a deathless hour
   with life or death I'd pay.

If I Can Rescue

If I can rescue with a rope of rhyme
   some beauty from the ruthless ruck of time
   and put it pulsing, singing from a frame
   of syllables that set a soul to flame—

If I can write a line however small
   of deathless beauty on life's wailing wall,
   I shall have made an answer to the cry
   of God in man—before my time to die.

II

James William Slater

You went as gently as a summer day
   goes golden down the distant river bend
   among the lessening hills
   with twilight like a petal-bosomed girl
   trailing an opal veil across the sky
   and in the deepening blue a rose-white star
   blooms tremulous.

I did not know our wealth till you were gone,
   your child-wife, then unknown to what life holds—

I took your priceless presence as a child
   takes mother, father, comrades, food and home—
   the way we take a long, long summer day,
   the balm and friendliness that men call June,
   with dawn on the hilltops, calling, singing dawn,
   wise trees in conference with indulgent clouds
   tempting the blaze of noon with shifting shade—
   soft rains on country roads and trooping flowers,
   farmers and horses drinking at the spring
   and children sailing little paper boats
   on pools that hold the blue and silver sky,
   all unaware that these dear values pass
   as day goes shimmering, shining down the river
   from dawn till noon, from noon to evening glow,

    with night's dark deep of suns and worlds aglow
    to cut our black bewilderment and loss
    with thoughts as sharp as knives
    or sweet as roses.

I did not know until your day was done
    how nobly fine it was, how swiftly gone—
    with over four score shadows falling ruefully
    on one so valiant in peace and war;
    how sane it was, how lovable its hates,
    and how you went like youth from dawn to dawn,
    escaping age,

      and leaving me to mourn.

Twilight After Rain

The west breaks suddenly translucent.

Sky and river meet in quivering ecstasy;
   the hills like happy hounds
     go leaping downward into sunset.

The sodden town that stood a listless sloven
   under rain-soaked trees
   airs every leaf,
   lifts newly-gilded spires
   and from her rain-washed windows flashes fire.

Gold lies on pavement pools—green gold—
   and sweet familiar grass wears artful green.

Children and dogs come running—
   mad-glad creatures
   freed from time and space,
   drinking green odor.

Birds call as to some far-flung dawn.

A thin sharp light invades the world,
   stabs into the heart of man
   a dagger of pure beauty....

"Nice, after the rain," is all he says.

A Whiff of Lilacs

A whiff of lilacs on the air
   can fill one with divine despair.

Today below my lonely room
   I saw a lilac bush in bloom—
   a blaze of green and purple flame—
   and suddenly I called your name.

Beloved, has life a breath more sweet,
   has heaven's happy valley
   a joy to match your rare heartbeat
   with mine in tender tally?

A whiff of lilacs in the rain—
   has heaven's cloudless weather
   a joy to match the human pain
   of life and love together?

III

Ballerina

May I not live too long
   for laughter, love and song—
may I not live to sit
bereft of will and wit,
until the nurses say,
"She's not so bright today—
she didn't seem to care
which way we did her hair,
and when an old beau came
she had forgot his name."

Oh, rather let them say,
   "She dressed and went quite gay,
in love with life and brave—
to dance upon her grave."
For she was dead at dawn,
her scarlet slippers on,
bequeathing us awhile
the shadow of a smile.

Butterfly

I am the worm
   that dared to dream
   a dream beyond belief—

I am the worm
   that made me a bed
   and lay in a silken sheaf—

I dreamed it deep
   and I dreamed it true
   that a worm might rise and fly—

That I would awake
   a flying flower
   in a blowing heaven of sky.

My Sycamore

When I awoke and saw her there
   wind-blown of all her leafy hair,
   wind-stripped to tattered underwear—
   my sycamore, a lithe young jade
   brought from the wild to bring me shade—

She said a lover from the wood,
   a ravening lover, fierce and rude,
   had seized and kissed her where she stood,
   kissed her to tatters, kissed her nude.

So there she stands—a wanton sight,
    her young limbs showing satin white
    beneath the rags of her delight.

October

She sits a valiant lady in despair
    before the taunting mirror of the year,
    rouges her cheeks, re-dyes her leafy hair
    and flaunts flamboyant skirts—to hide her fear.

Upon the dimming outline of her lips
    she paints a scarlet pattern of a smile,
    emblazons on her frosted fingertips
    enamelings of oriental guile.

Submissive to the kisses of the sun
    to win the gauds and glamours he bestows,
    she rises shedding jewels one by one
    to walk in robes of amber, umber, rose.

Along the hills she trails a lovely lie,
    faithful to beauty at her latest breath,
    endeavoring, although about to die,
    to fashion beauty for the face of death.

The Pool

The day—the day—the shining day
   when happy winds were blowing
   and down the shady garden way
   the cherry flowers were snowing—

I blew and blew the wide world through
   all whispering wet and cool,
   and saw the high, the silver sky
   down in a pavement pool.

I leaned to see the trees and me
   and clouds a-blowing by—
   then blew away for fear I'd stay
   and fall into the sky!—

The day—the day—the shining day
   when happy winds were blowing
   and down the shady garden way
   the cherry flowers were snowing.

Indian Summer

While gray November longed for summer days
    gone shining, showering by,
      for dawn and noon and twilight's tender ways
    of dallying down the sky,

Back to her lap crept all the lovely three
    with whisper, kiss and sigh,
      trailing a rose, a bird, a drowsy bee,
    a last lone butterfly.

Event

He wore a rose and a crown of gold
    and wings on his feet that flew—
    the light in his eyes was eons old,
    the song on his lips was new.

He came by the secret gate of birth
    on a seven-summered sigh
    of ecstasy with the greening earth
    and the wonder of the sky—

He went by the secret gate of death
    when the flying feet fell slow
    and the lilt of the dawn in his April breath
    was lost in a May-day snow—

A rose he wore and a crown of gold
   and wings on his feet that flew;
   the light in his eyes was eons old,
   the song on his lips was new.

He was the rose for glowing, he was the wind for going,
   his breath was honey blowing from the hearts of
      widening flowers
   he was the bird for singing, for flying, flashing, swinging,
   his laughter was the ringing of the early woodland hours—

He was sunshine, he was shadow, he was the rain upon the meadow
   when the clover's high and redolent of nectar for the bees,
   the dawn for glint and gleaming, the noon for blaze and
      beaming,
   and twilight lay a-dreaming in his eyes like purple seas—

He was the star for burning, the moon for wonder, yearning,
   and eon-deeps of learning looked outward at his birth—
   he was the soul-flower knowing, all free for coming, going,
   the man-god, leaping, growing in the garden of the earth.

          *   *   *

Peach blow, cherry snow, apple blossoms strewing
   petal paths for running down the old earth-way,
   Maytime, playtime, with your skies a-blueing
   and your robins ringing out a roundelay,
   tell me, lovely springtime, lilting, laughing wingtime,
   where's the lovely laughing mate with whom you used to play?

Saint Joseph's

Time and the river have their way—
   Saint Joseph's tower comes down today.
   No more the Easter moon and I
   shall see that beauty etch the sky.

Time and the river have their will—
   Saint Joseph's bell is mute and still.
   No more the Easter thoroughfare
   shall hear that music etch the air.

Twilight shall faint upon the loss
   from heaven of the golden cross
   that tipped Saint Joseph's slender finger
   where dawn and sunset loved to linger.

Time and the river have their way—
   Saint Joseph's tower comes down today,
   yet time and tide shall not erase
   that memory of beauty's face.

Barefoot Sandals

Ah, little barefoot sandals brown and still,
   do you long to be a-roaming on the hill,
   flashing down the garden way,
   fellows with the wind at play—
   are you weary waiting, wistful, silent, chill?

When morning mounts and makes the old world sweet
   with the lilt of laughing children in the street,
   do you ache to join them there
   to be twinkling down the stair
   to the darling, dancing gladness of her feet?

Do you know the asters troop in purple gloom
   too late to greet the love that bade them bloom—
   that they seem to watch and wait
   at the lonely garden gate
   while you weary in the little upper room?

Ah, hapless little shoes that held my all,
   my joy of life within your trappings small,
   where's the lithe and lovely thing
   that each morning lent you wing?
   Are you weary waiting wingless for her call?

Brenda Passes

She came like morning
   eager, blue-gold, tender,
   breathing glad light
   unconscious of her splendor.

Young love she met
   along an April way
   where rolls the greening earth
   from night to day,

And at the imploring
   magic of his smile
   she walked with him
   a lovely lilac mile,

When suddenly
   bespoken for some noon
   beyond the byway
   of the earth and moon,

Wanting to stay,
   reluctant to surrender,
   she went away
   unconscious of her splendor.

Lilacs

Lilacs again down the old earth way
   greening, blueing, blowing—
   so sweet their breath
   so short their stay
   so swift their coming, going.

Lilacs lush at the kitchen pane
   wet winds and a robin calling
   again the ruthless lash of rain
   the drift of petals falling.

Lilacs marching along the lane
   with purple pennons flying,
   again the pang—the lilac pain
   of beauty breathing—dying.

      *   *   *

Lilacs again—and you away
   who brought me their first bloom—
   sad-glad lilacs bravely gay
   in our empty upper room.

When Spring Comes Down to Shottery

When spring comes down to Shottery
　in England, greening England,
　with April's lovely lottery
　of song and shine and shower,
　when honeybees begin to sup
　in honey-blowing England,
　and broideries of buttercup
　set all the fields a-flower,

It's golden time, it's golden time
　in England, greening England,
　and love as in the olden time
　comes out to walk with May,
　dream-deep in love's own lottery,
　young love, in lilting England,
　across the fields to Shottery
　and sweet Anne Hathaway!

At Easter

White hyacinths arrive serene
   with fronded fingers curled
   around their Easter offering
   of beauty to the world.

Mutely they beckon us to share
   what heaven bids them bring
   to let our eager nostrils know
   an ecstasy of spring.

In virgin loveliness they rise
   at April's opening door
   distilling petal pleas of peace
   into a world of war.

      *   *   *

So Jesus rises, blooms and dies
   into immortal birth
   shedding the light of brotherhood
   upon a blundering earth.

Nirvana

High on a hilltop now I want to lie
   on grasses cool with memories of dew,
   looking through leafy windows to the sky
   and drowsy doorways breezing into blue.

On hilltop grasses spread from blue to blue,
   a solitary passenger at sea,
   I want to lie with only dreams to do
   and feel my earth-ship sailing silently.

All through the sheer September afternoon,
   my grassy deck spread soft from blue to blue,
   I want to lie and wait there for the moon,
   truant of life—with only dreams to do.

Resurrection

Behold the morning of the year
   when beauty comes to birth—
   with petal lips and fronds unfurled
   she walks the waiting earth

In dandelion petticoat,
   a scarf of blowing blue,
   a robin singing in her throat,
   a crocus in her shoe.

Enchanted at a butterfly
   alighting on her vest,
   a throb, a pulse, an infant's cry
   newborn within her breast,

She combs her hair with April rain
   and laughs a lilac breath,
   aware, in spite of war and pain,
   that life is lord of death.

The Mother

In all the golden glint of June,
    the minstrelsy of bird and brook and tree,
    my heart's in flower, my soul's in tune—
    a human blossom blooms alone for me!

In all the carnival of joy
    I nestle softly to my wondering breast
    my miracle—my breathing boy—
    amazed that mortal arms should be so blest.

Sweet wonder, open now your eyes,
    lucent as morning on a purple sea—
    oh, happiest day of all beneath the skies
    that dawns on love's triumphant trinity!

Through a Cool Green Gateway

Through a cool green gateway in the hill
   where the road lies sylvan, sweet and still
   to the Vale of Sleeping,

They bore the slender sheath of you
   in white, white rest, with a rose or two
   in waxen keeping.

But where were you, alas, the while—
   the wilding you of the rebel smile
   with faith upleaping?

Shiela

The moon has spread her silver bed
  so still and white and high
  for tired little stars that tread
  the wide and wondrous sky—
    sleep, Shiela, like a sleepy star
    here in your mother's breast,
    for all the sleepy stars that are
    take not so sweet a rest.

On the shadowy wall the sparrows all
  beneath the ivy hid,
  make many a jostling plaint and brawl,
  close many a drowsy lid—
    sleep, Shiela, like a sleepy bird
    here in your mother's breast,
    for never bird ear ever heard
    took half so safe a rest.

In the garden where the flowers fair
  breathe odors to the moon,
  prone on the path deserted there
  your doll lies in a swoon—
    sleep, Shiela, my own deathless doll,
    here in your mother's breast,
    for star nor bird nor doll nor all
    were ever half so blest.

The Easter Child

I looked on Easter hyacinths new-risen,
   white stars from cells of clay—
   and learned that life had ushered from a prison
   your miracle, today—

A child-flower, dewy-sweet and human-hearted,
   and lighted like a star,
   a hungry little venturer newly started
   for journeyings afar—

And thought—the light that sets a soul to burning
   from the unseen, unknown,
   must hold the power to satisfy its yearning
   and bring it to its own.

Oh, For a Ship

Oh, for a ship and a wind that's true
   and a dream to steer me by,
     through the scudding clouds to the breathing blue
   of the upper April sky!

Away from houses row on row
   blind to the stars and the afterglow,
   holding the soul to the snare of things
   while morning blooms and blows and sings—
   away from headlines—horrors, news,
   arguments, trials, preachings, pews,
   the little man with his little god,
   the millionaire, the man with the hod,
   the man with a crown, the man with a queue,
   heathen, pagan, Christian, Jew—
   the men with guns, the tanks, the trenches,
   prisons, ship holds, foxholes, stenches—
   up and away, oh, man with wings,
   up from tyranny of things,
   the blundering tribes, the troubled sod
   for a crystal breath in the blue of God!

A ship and a dream and an April day
   and an early hour for going
   from the reeling earth away—away
   with the soft wet breezes blowing.

The Prince of the Ragged School

In a crooked byway
   of dear old London town
   I met a little Eton boy
   with big eyes bright and brown—
   his hat was tall and shiny,
   his jacket short and trim;
   his shoes cut low let his stockings show
   though his trousers were long for him.

I bit my lip for smiling
   at his tiny cane held high,
   when near him on a corner,
   with a twinkle in his eye,
   a shabby little urchin
   with blacking brush and stool
   said, "Shine, sir, shine? If you will you may dine
   with the Prince of the Ragged School."

The way of the world. Here's a palace
   with a cradle lined with wool,
   while there is a grimy hovel
   where the cradle is too full—
   so one shall go to Eton
   and teach mankind to rule,
   while the cornerstone makes a windy throne
   for the Prince of the Ragged School.

The Guest

So little have I known of power or pelf—
    a little rented nest, a bed, a shelf,
    a place to put a doll, a book, a chair—
    yet all that heaven has offered blossomed there.

I worked and sang and laughed the hours away,
    enamored of the game—the mother-play—
    my lilting mate and mocker fairy-sweet,
    a miracle of joy on twinkling feet,

Until a guest came creeping at my door
    unseen, unknown. I play the game no more—
    the gladdest since a human flower unfurled,
    the saddest—since the making of the world.

Blind Girl

When last I saw her young and lovely, sleeping
    the sleep too deep for breath,
  with all the sad-glad roses round her keeping
    her bridal tryst with death,

When I recalled her hunger after beauty—
    who could not see the skies,
  her search courageous for some fitting duty—
    a veil before her eyes,

And how she tried to see the hills, the river,
    friends and each friendly place,
  the sunset glow, the evening star a-quiver,
    dawn—and her mother's face—

I wept. And yet I felt a sound of singing,
    a far-flung minstrelsy
  of voices, many voices, ringing—
    The veil is gone—she's free! . . .

And when on still, swift wheels we followed after
    the petal girl beneath a quilt of rose,
  I felt her following, too, with running laughter,
    a glad young ghost on dancing toes.

Burbank

He who conspired with sun, seed, sod,
   till finer forms arose,
   did he not live the life of God
in earth's green garden close?

Who sowed his thought and stirred the clod
   to serve a human need,
   did he not live the love of God
in faith, in hope, in deed?

Father Cotter

The bells of St. Lawrence
  ring out on the air
  solemnly calling
  the people to prayer,

Morning bells, evening bells
  down through the years,
  weeping bells, wedding bells
  smiling through tears,

Christmas bells gladly
  announcing the birth
  of Jesus, the Christ-child,
  the Saviour of earth,

Easter bells ringing
  release from death's prison—
  the stone rolls away,
  the Saviour arisen—

While down through the years
  in service unending
  her strong loyal son
  stands erect and attending

The candle of faith
  in devotion sublime,
  beloved and revered
  and unconquered by time.

The bells of St. Lawrence
  bespeak him today
  what hearts cannot utter
  and words cannot say.

John Campbell

A Portrait

When I was a girl in a gala gown—
    before the Old World toppled down,
    when Europe sat on gilded thrones
    unmindful of time's undertones,
    while kings slept on and steeples pealed
    and no one dreamed of Flanders Field
    or of the all-awakening date
    of hapless Hiroshima's fate—

When I was a girl in a gala gown
    I saw the father of our town
    walking alone down Center Street
    erect, alert, on sturdy feet,
    with massive head and shoulders broad—
    a master of the ground he trod,
    an aging giant in a cloak
    gripping a giant staff of oak.

He was grave and worn. I was gay and young,
    my life unlived, my song unsung.
    He had wooed the hills of iron and coal,
    begot a city, reached a goal;
    and now on his last, lusty mile
    he paused, and wooed me with a smile—
    a smile that held a warm caress
    for youth and hope and happiness.

* * *

Since I was a girl in a gala gown
   old London Bridge has fallen down;
   earth shudders at the blundering pack
   of gods and devils on her back,
   yet—though my hour grows grim and late—
   a nobleman still walks in state
   and sends a heartening smile to me
   across the miles of history.

Old Aleck

I'm glad they built it broad and low—
   the Courthouse wall, where he may go,
   now that he's old and on relief,
   to sit awhile and smile at grief.

God made him black—as black as night,
   a slave—where all the gods were white,
   and when set free he didn't know
   just what to do or where to go,
   for even freedom needs a pole
   by which to navigate the soul.

Unlike the wise men from afar,
   heaven held for him no special star,
   yet somehow on a northering trail
   he shuffled into Irondale,
   and somehow earned his humble way
   long laboring years, until today,
   battered and bearded like a goat,
   a mellow music in his throat,
   a mellow magic in his eye,
   he doffs and smiles as I pass by.

He's on relief. The white gods think
   it wrong that he should spend for drink—
   but were it not a point too fine
   to grudge an Omar of his wine
   the last few days before he dies
   and shuffles into paradise?

I'm glad they built it broad and low,
   the Courthouse wall, where he may go,
   an ancient Omar on relief,
   to invite his soul and smile at grief.

When Lisa Sang at Carnegie

When Lisa sang at Carnegie,
   mistress of rote and rule,
   enchantment rose to ecstasy—
   while I, a sad-glad fool,
   remembered how she sang for me
   before she knew a note,
   out of a wildwood anarchy
   of birdlings in her throat—
   out of a springtime revelry
   of birdlings in her throat.

Baby Nancy

I saw her once and suddenly
   I knew what beauty ought to be.

What gods conspired to dream and do
   a poem wonderful as you?

What fortunate creative fancy
   begot the poem Nancy

To taunt aspiring human fools
   to capture with iambic tools

The lingering light of paradise
   that dazzles us in Nancy's eyes?

When Her Ship Comes In

Gran just smiled at little Meg
   one day when she hurt her leg—
   "Hush, don't cry, come sit by me;
   when my ship comes in, you'll see,
   there shall be a doll so fair,
   other girls will come to stare!"

And once when I burst out crying
   b'cause my little pup was dying,
   Gran just held me on her knee—
   "When my ship comes in, you'll see,
   there shall be a target gun
   for a boy who prays for one."

Sometimes when Kate sits and sews
   great big tears roll down her nose—
   Gran just smiles at Meg and me.
   "When my ship comes in, you'll see,
   Kate shall have a satin gown
   just to match her curls so brown!"

Sometimes I pretend at night,
   after Gran has dimmed the light,
   that her ship's come, loaded down,
   full of things for all the town—
   that we're rich as rich can be,
   cakes for breakfast, dinner, tea!

We won't spread our bread so thin
   when her ship comes sailing in.

Autumn Leaves

Up and down
up and down
   little ghosts run through the town,
   up the streets
   and down the alleys
   on the hills
   and in the valleys.

Up and down
up and down
   little ghosts all thin and brown,
   whispering, whispering together
   in the windy autumn weather!

Dogwood

Out of the dream of winter woodland hours,
   the year's long night,
   the dogwood dawns into a thousand flowers
   suddenly white,

A bride arrayed in virgin veils and laces
   tenderly gay
   and glad, among the trooping forest graces
   that hedge her way.

What the Summer Said

"I must be sleeping," the summer said;
  "let me lie down in my leafy bed—
  gentle snow
  breathe and blow
  weave a white coverlet for my head—
  a soft white coverlet for my head.

"When April breezes blow blue and fair
  robins will waken me slumbering there—
  I'll arise
  I'll arise
  wearing a rose in my cool green hair—
  a reddening rose in my cool green hair."

Snowing

Snowing
Snowing
   soft and deep
   all night long as I lay asleep—

Snowing
Snowing
   soft and still
   piling high on the window sill—

All the world is white and new;
   nobody's ever walked it through!

The old, old plum tree black and bare
   is an old, old woman with snowy hair
   leaning against the garden wall
   wearing a snowy shoulder shawl—

All the world is white and new;
   I'll be the first to walk it through!

November

Today I heard a thrushy note
   out of November's husky throat—
   a lilt of some young wanton thing
   amid a solemn gathering.

My lazy lady sycamore
   shed summer rags around the door—
   lifted her lithe limbs to the air,
   shameless in ragged underwear.

And when I treaded sylvan places
   strewn with her sisters' tattered laces,
   I saw one leaning naked, cool,
   and white, above a woodland pool.

Plum Tree

The old, old plum tree
   black and bent,
   propped by the garden wall—
   an old, old woman
   worn and spent
   has heard a robin's call—
   and roused to April vanity
   has put on a flowery shawl,
   a flaunting flowery shawl.

Rose

What is this happening we call the rose—
    a rocket rising from the garden close
    exploding, spilling beauty on the air
    as if to spill it were its only care—
    exhaling one divine, delicious breath
    before it showers in slow and lovely death?

At dawn I caught a rose's tender glow
    and ran to it as though a rose might know—
    as though the willing petals of its purse
    might give a secret of the universe,
    so deep its heart, so pure its tear,
    if only it had tongue, or I had ear,
    as though when first the whirl of worlds began,
    one chose to venture rose-ward, one toward man,
    as though, along a path each might have missed,
    dawn drew us to a dim-remembered tryst—

Robin

Up from a shell
  of shattered blue
  throbbing
  thrusting
  bursting through—

  a scarlet flash
  a dart of wings
  a gush of melody
  that flings

  a call of love
  a crystal cry

  a rocket
  ravishing the sky—

Bee

I am a summer rover—
   on sweets I dine and sup
   and every blowing clover
   becomes my drinking cup.

When from a flowery chalice
   a treasure sweet I glean
   I fly to my waxen palace
   and serve it to my queen.

I am a summer rover—
   into many a flower I creep
   and when the summer's over
   I fly straight home to sleep.

Dandelion

Shaggy yellow imp
   glad unwelcome comer
   ragamuffin mummer
   on the lawn of summer—

Irrepressible star
   defying rake and hoer
   laughing at man the mower
   smiling with God the sower—

Winter River

The river, the shimmering river, is dead—
    white-lidded, white-bosomed, she lies in her bed,
    she sees not her sad sister hills standing by,
    she heeds not her sorrowing mother, the sky,
    and her soft silvery feet that delighted to run
    through the far western gate to her lover, the sun,
    are shrouded and still as the feet of the old—
    her lover is gone,
    his love has grown cold.

His jewels of dawn she has dropped from her sleeve,
    the diamond of noonday, the opal of eve,
    his gift of a star, the white brooch of a moon
    she has lost and forgotten—so deep is her swoon—
    nor cares she—so proud and so cold is her rest—
    that small human creatures are treading her breast,
    for her glad heart is still as a heart that is old—
    her lover is gone,
    his love has grown cold.

April Snow

Petal-soft and still they fall
   disappearing
   disappearing—
   lovely ghosts that mutely call
   to the unhearing.

The warm earth drinks them eagerly
   conceiving roses
   pale wild roses
   opening gaily, silently
   in woodland closes.

September

When leafy days
   go whispering, blue,
   rain-cool yet kissed with fire,

   their lovelinesses
   stir anew
   the heart's divine desire

   to capture beauty
   in a net
   of words beyond decay—

   to fathom why
   the stage is set
   and what the immortal play.

The Flying Fish

Where sea and sky are dreaming
   in azure mystery
   upflashes, glinting, gleaming,
   the sun-bird of the sea.

From his nether fellows straying,
   in the nether waters playing
   he arises maying, maying
   to the ether ecstasy,

A mystic venturer trying
   with a passion deep, undying
   for the leap, the flash, the flying
   into blue infinity!

And, lo, from his upsoaring
   on momentary wing
   comes the skylark's sweet outpouring,
   that joying, heavenward thing

From height to height aspiring
   on wings unspent, untiring
   and the myriad choiring, choiring
   of the birdfolk in the spring!

Sea Shell

I come from the sea,
   my mother the sea—
   I leaped from her lap to the shore,
   and now I hear her calling me—
   calling forevermore.

In the soft sea sand,
   the friendly sand,
   I lie in a dreamy doze—
   a beautiful thing,
   a wonderful thing
   with a lip like an opening rose.

Hold me close to your ear
   and see if you hear
   the voice of my mother implore,
   for my mother the sea
   is calling me—calling forevermore.

Pasadena

A little house in Bonnie Street
   a rose-grown wooden nest
   with mountains in the twilight
   marching west.

A star above a palm tree
   tender, tremulous, high,
   watching a young indifferent moon
   in the lower sky—
   a slender stripling of a moon
   in a cool green sky.

A passionate star, a listless moon,
   a palm tree's friendly tower,
   the still, cold breath of the canyon
   in the twilight hour—
   the breath of the Mother Mountains
   in the twilight hour,

And up from the darkening planet
   a gush of melody,
   the fountain song of the mockingbird
   playing momently—
   the laugh of a hidden mocker
   insolent, joying, free.

Broadway

Broadway—Broadway—
   when the night comes on
   and you flash your million stars
   for men to gaze upon,

And when like children straying
   they crowd your great white way,
   enchanted into staying
   where night is bright as day—

When they're dancing, crooning, singing,
   when they're prancing, mooning, swinging
   to the beating of the brasses and the blare,
   when old memories come stinging
   and with wine and song they're flinging
   gay defiance at tomorrow and its care—

Do you ever think or dream
   of springtime nights gone by
   when you were just a meadow path
   beneath a starlit sky,
   when springtime odors filled the air
   from blossoms wet with dew,
   when you wore violets in your hair
   and life and love were new?

Broadway—Broadway—
   do you ever groan
   and ache for beauty buried
   beneath your paving stone?
   Do you ever sigh
   and wish you were a lover's lane
   beneath a starlit sky?

The Goldfish

I am a tiny goldfish
   and anyone can see
   that all of my relations
   live in a bowl with me.

Somebody feeds us every day
   and keeps us fresh and clean,
   but I heard my grandmother say
   it's really very mean

To keep us prisoners in a bowl
   with no new place to swim;
   and I heard my grandfather say
   that an old, old fish told him

A million, million fishes
   are swimming in the sea,
   and some are big as elephants
   and some are small like me.

Motoring

The day—a blue-white diamond of the year
   with every facet burning;
   the way—a lure from lovelinesses near
   to dreams beyond the turning.

We follow singing dawn's delightful feet
   through wakened morning-glories—
   her way brings children trooping dewy-sweet
   with wonder at her stories;

We mount the jeweled blue of noon ablaze,
   and thread her woodland valleys,
   descending soft by cool and purple ways
   through shining, shadowy valleys,

Along the golden lane to sunset gate,
   flung high in ruby splendor,
   and by a lucent river homing late
   'neath evening's opal tender,

Till up the azure east a white world strays,
   alone, all lustrous, glowing,
   herald of midnight suns and glinting ways
   of worlds beyond our knowing!

The Wind

Up and down the world I go,
    warm as summer, cold as snow,
    north and south and east and west,
    wandering, wandering without rest.

I rush across the seven seas;
    I whisper to a thousand trees—
    up where the hilltop grasses grow
    I sing a song that is soft and low.

I run with you through the pouring rain,
    I laugh at the door, I tap at the pane,
    I dance with you, I sigh and creep
    and kiss you as you lie asleep.

Up and down the world I go,
    warm as summer, cold as snow,
    day and night in every spot
    I play with you and you see me not.

The Tree

I stand a prisoner from my birth;
   through every night and day
   my feet are fastened in the earth—
   I cannot walk away.

So year by year I stretch and strain
   to reach the summer sky;
   loved by the sun, the wind, the rain,
   I never cease to try.

I have a hundred arms to fling
   my blossoms to the air,
   a hundred birds to flash and swing
   and nestle in my hair.

I have a brooklet cool and clear;
   I have a purple shade
   where children come from far and near
   to climb and splash and wade.

But I'm a prisoner from my birth;
   through every night and day
   my feet are fastened in the earth—
   I cannot walk away.

IV

When Father Cotter Rings the Bells

When Father Cotter rings the bells
   he's ringing in the day.
    The sun comes up. I wake and dress
    and run outdoors to play—
    but the old church holds its finger high
    and tries all day to touch the sky!

When Father Cotter rings the bells
   he's ringing out the light.
    The sun goes down. I say my prayers
    and sleep all through the night—
    but the old church stretches high and far
    and tries all night to touch a star!

The Elm Tree

When summer comes to Irondale
   the streets are cool and shady—
   the old, old elm tree by the road
   looks like a stately lady.

She draws her skirt along the ground—
   I stepped on it today—
   and patiently and gracefully
   she tries to walk away.

She must have tried a hundred years
   to set herself as free
   as frogs or birds or flying squirrels
   or a boy who climbs like me.

And there's a man in Irondale,
   they say he is a loon—
   he likes to lie on Sunrise Hill
   and wait there for the moon.

He'd rather die than be a tree
   to have to stand and stay
   forever in the same old place
   and never get away.

The Great House in the Square

The door swings wide on the threshold
   of the great house in the square—
   the house with the grim green shutters
   and silence everywhere—
   the garden lies a wildwood
   of blooms where the roses rare
   are waiting the foot of childhood
   to find its kingdom there.
   The door swings wide on the threshold
   of the great house in the square.

Age sits in the lonely parlor
   of the great house in the square
   with youth that aches and paces
   and listens at the stair,
   for their hearts are a pagan wildwood
   of love and hope and care
   lest motherhood and childhood
   should miss their kingdom there.
   Age waits with youth in the parlor
   of the great house in the square.

A guest has come in the twilight
   to the great house in the square—
   fling high the grim green shutters,
   chase silence anywhere—
   a voice for the garden wildwood,
   a hand for the roses rare,
   for the leaping foot of childhood
   has found a kingdom there—
   Emmy Lou has come in the twilight
   to the great house in the square.

To a Child

Only God could dream and write
  a poem beautiful as night—
  a drift of stars that sing and say,
  a planet flushing into day.

Only God could dream and sing
  a poem exquisite as spring—
  a drift of green that breathes and blows
  into a robin or a rose.

Only God could dream and do
  a poem wonderful as you—
  a child who loves, laughs, sings and knows
  more than a star, a bird, a rose.

The Venturer

I saw him start to school today—
  the little boy across the way.
  He's six, and proudly put his plan
  to start alone—just like a man.

I saw his mother standing there,
  smiling through tears he did not share,
  watching the boy with eye that shone
  plunge into life to swim alone.

Awhile she stood and watched him fare
   until he turned around the square,
   flesh of her flesh, bone of her bone—
   then went into the house alone.

The First Day at School

Ma, 'tain't no use for me to go—
   she don't teach nothin' that I know!

She talks about the birds an' bees
   'n' never mentions A B Cs—
   sings 'bout the fishes in the brooks
   'n' says I needn't bring no books!

'N' when I told my name was Ted,
   what d'you think she went and said?—
   "Your really name is Theodore,
   so we won't call you Ted no more!"

* * *

So when she marched us out to play,
   I 'cided I'd come home to stay—
   for 'tain't no use for me to go—
   she don't teach nothin' that I know.

The Scholar

I used to think the world was flat—
　with a great big place to fall off at!

From Grandma's garden on the river
　I watched the water flow forever
　and thought, "Far down the river bend
　is where the world comes to an end!"

I thought the hills all green and brown
　were just God's fences round the town
　built strong and high against the sky
　so that the moon could not get by,
　to make a place for cows and clover—
　and keep us all from blowing over!

That's why I would not climb until
　I reached the top of Sunrise Hill—
　would you, if you thought the world was flat
　with a great, high place to fall off at?

* * *

I'm braver than I used to be,
　for now I study geography,
　and know the world is just a ball
　with gravity to hold us all.

A person's missed a lot if he
　has never studied geography—
　what made me such a fraidy-cat
　was that big place to fall off at.

You'd Better Eat Your Dinner

You'd better eat your dinner
   and feel all fat and full
   of milk and bread and butter
   before you go to school.

For once there was a little girl
   who wouldn't eat her dinner,
   till they could count her little ribs—
   and she kept getting thinner!

They dressed her in a furry coat,
   but everyone who knew her
   was thinking, "When the summer comes
   the breeze will blow right through her,

"And like the dandelion ball
   she'll grow all thin and gray
   and some day when the wind gets up
   she'll all be blown away."

You'd better eat your dinner
   and feel all fat and full
   of milk and bread and butter
   before you go to school.

On Mother's Wedding Day

Sometimes it makes me lonesome
　to think I wasn't there—
　not even in the playroom
　or listening at the stair—
　that I wasn't anywhere!

I didn't see the presents
　all laid out in a row
　or watch them mix the wedding cake
　or taste the lovely dough—
　I wasn't born, and so

I couldn't be the flower girl
　on mother's wedding day
　and walk behind her down the aisle
　and hear the organ play—
　I just had to stay away.

And yet—it makes me lonesome
　to think I wasn't there—
　not even in the playroom,
　in the pantry—on the stair—
　that I wasn't anywhere.

As Janet Dances

Say, Moon,
    are you ever jealous of the sun
    because he shines so bright
    he makes the day?

Oh, don't be jealous, Moon!
    The sun is hot and red as fire—
    the stars run off from him
    and children run to the shade.
    But you are cool and kind and white;
    children and stars come out to play with you
    and stay up late to talk and dance and twinkle.

Say, Moon,
    are you a large and shining pearl
    with little diamond stars set round
    like mother's ring?

Who wears you on her finger, lovely Moon?

The Lake

Once
   when I ran to the shore in the morning
   the sun was not out,
   the sky was all gray,
   and the lake was a river,
   a hurrying river—
   it would not stay with me or play.

And once
   when the world was all shining and blowing,
   the lake was a lady;
   her dress was dark blue
   with all of her pretty white petticoats showing!
   I played it was true
   and nobody knew.

And once
   when I sat there all tired and quiet
   and watching the sun-fire go down in the west,
   the lake was a rainbow,
   a still, melting rainbow—
   I like it the best.
   I like it the best.

The Sandman

When the lamps burn red
  and the table's spread
  and it's time for the purple plums,
Tommy Tinker's eyes
  grow big and wise—
  for that's when the Sandman comes.

From his big high chair
  he tries to stare
  and pretend he's wide awake,
but his hand falls soon
  and he drops his spoon,
  and the Sandman gets his cake,

And his buttered buns
  where the jelly runs
  rosy red as a jell should be,
and the last sweet sup
  from his silver cup
  of drowsy cambric tea.

     *   *   *

Ah, my sleepy boy,
  I am sad with joy,
  I am glad with a pain that fears—
in my mother's breast
  I would keep your nest
  for the Sandman of the years.

That Bold Baby Donna

That bold baby Donna
   has kicked off her shoe;
   she wants to go barefoot
   and roam the world through,

Away from her mother
   on little bare feet
   with nothing to wear
   and nothing to eat.

She wants to go straying
   before she can walk;
   she wants to go playing
   before she can talk.

She wants to go running
   with children to school;
   she wants to go swimming
   with fish in the pool.

She wants to go flying
   like birds in the air
   before she can climb up
   or crawl down the stair.

That bold baby Donna
   can just crow and coo,
   clap, gurgle and laugh
   and kick off her shoe.

At the Font

Hail, lovely Isabella Lee,
    fresh flower from fields of Arcady
    with love-winds blowing—

Hail, trusting tremulous human star
    kindled with light from high and far
    beyond our knowing—

Breathe fragrance, burn in joy for those
    who wistful watch thy star and rose
    divinely growing—

Breathe forth the faith that dares the years;
    burn with a light that fires the seers
    divinely glowing—

Rise, lovely Isabella Lee,
    white star of time's infinity
    where'er you're going—

Arise to high humanity,
    rise though the height bring Calvary—
    your service showing.

I Wonder

I wonder what I used to do
   before I came to stay
   and be your little boy, Mother,
   and what I did all day?

I wonder who took care of me
   and how I cared to play
   if I lived off somewhere in heaven,
   with you so far away.

I can't remember how it was
   or anyone I knew,
   but think I must have cried and cried
   to come down here to you.

Rain

The garden is wet. The window vine shivers
    and tears from the sky on the cold window pane
    are running like rivers,
    like dear little rivers—
    my father and mother have gone on the train.

Ever and ever so far they are going—
    over the mountains and down to the sea.
    The wet wind is blowing,
    the wet leaves are snowing
    out there in the rain
    from the sycamore tree.

Ever and ever so far they are flying—
    no robin is singing,
    no cat-bird or thrush.
    The whole world is crying!
    My old doll is lying
    out there in the rain by the wet lilac bush.

Measles

The bedroom's dark, it seems like night
   except for little PEEP-o-LIGHT
   that Mother has not shut away.
   He runs right down a golden lane
   and dances on my counterpane
   and says, "Will you come out and play?"

He leaps into the water jar
   and twinkles at me like a star!
   While Mother reads of ogres grim,
   he winks, "That story isn't true!
   Come out! The sky and pool are blue!
   Come out! Will you come out and swim?"

He's lit a lantern red and bright,
   that pretty little PEEP-o-LIGHT,
   and sits on Mother's wedding ring—
   I wish he wouldn't beckon so,
   for I'm too hot and tired to go
   and play or swim or anything.

The Locomotive

I am a giant black and strong—
   my food is fire, my tail is long!

I go rushing—bellowing—crying—
   my smoky breath behind me flying.

I push through mountains as high as the sky;
   I light the dark with my terrible eye.

I plunge into hollows and under the hill;
   I thunder through valleys all peaceful and still.

I whistle and shriek to the children at play
   to look out for me and keep out of my way.

And when in bed you are safely curled,
   you hear me wailing around the world.

On the Stoop

I wouldn't like to be a star
 so high and white and fine
 with never anything to do
 but shine and shine and shine.

I wouldn't like to be a moon
 so high and silver-pale
 with never anything to do
 but sail and sail and sail.

I'd rather be a little girl
 or boy—like me and you—
 with always some new games to play
 and some new things to do.

The Live Doll

That little girl around the square,
   the one that never combs her hair,
   has got exactly what I wanted,
   and made me dreadful disappointed—
   old Santa left it Christmas morning
   without a single word of warning!

She says she doesn't care at all
   about my beautiful new doll—
   she says my doll's an old dead thing
   that cannot cry or hear me sing—
   that hers is live as live can be,
   with really eyes that really see,
   with hands that hold your finger tight,
   and real toenails—ten, all right—
   with cheeks all pink and soft as silk
   and lips that really cry for milk!

Soon as her daddy gets his pay,
   they'll buy a go-cart right away,
   and when the weather's dry and fair
   she's going to push it round the square!

She didn't ask for it at all,
   and yet she got that real live doll.

The Wanderer

Today I felt so very bad
   I left my mother and my dad,
   my sisters Mary, Rose and Sue,
   and everyone I ever knew—
   for since we've got that brand-new brother
   they all forget me—even Mother.

I walked a hundred miles away
   to show them all how long I'd stay
   and let them see how sad they'd be
   if anyone should kidnap me.

The world grew cool—the world grew dark—
   and everybody left the park.
   "Time to go home," the watchman said.
   "The swans and ducks have gone to bed,
   and every little girl alive
   should be at home by half past five."

It seemed a hundred years or two
   since I'd seen anyone I knew,
   so I went hurrying home to see
   if anyone remembered me
   and there the house stood just the same,
   the same old street, the same old name,
   the same old dog, the same old cat,
   the same old door, the same old mat,
   the same old table set for tea,
   and no one even noticed me—
   the same old teapot on the tray—
   and no one knew I'd been away.

I Made Some Hills Against a Sky

I made some hills against a sky
   on my new crayon pad;
   I made a golden river flow—
   it made me feel so glad

to see the hills and river,
   I couldn't stop to play—
   I made some grass and trees and flowers
   along a purple way.

I made some shaggy sycamores
   like ours in Irondale
   and down the golden river
   I made a steamboat sail.

I made some houses in a row
   with pavements white and neat—
   I made my great-grandmother
   go walking down the street!

She always sits upstairs in bed,
   wearing a cap and shawl,
   and if it hadn't been for me
   she'd never walk at all.

I'm Making Me an Airship

I'm making me an airship
   as fast as forty cars,
   and I'll go flying up the sky
   to see who lights the stars.

And early in the morning
   when no one stirs about
   I'll go up in my flying ship
   to see who puts them out.

Bed Time

The moon's a boat—a silver boat—
   the sky's a deep blue sea,
   and one white star—a lonely star—
   is calling down to me,

"Don't go to bed! Don't go to bed!
   if you'll come up and play
   I'll let you sail my silver boat
   to where night meets the day!"

Star, star, high and white,
   let down a rope of light—
   and up the purple night
   I'll climb to you!

Grandfather's House

Grandfather's house is big and still
   with ice cream every day—
   but never any boy or girl
   to talk to me or play.

The parlor chairs are dressed in white
   like ladies at a party—
   but when I marched them in a row
   the maid said, "Naughty Marty!"

And once when I was crying loud
   away off up the stair
   Grandfather crawled out to the hall
   and played he was a bear!

He growled—but Mother smiled, and I
   kept quiet as a mouse
   and listened to him roar—"What's that!
   No crying in this house!"

On Hallowe'en

On Hallowe'en, on Hallowe'en
   when witches ride and croon
   and big black bats come flying
   across a frightened moon—

When wild winds whip the sycamore
   and scare the leaves away,
   when giants, dwarfs and ogres
   come out to dance and play—

I'm going to be a goblin
   and act as goblins should,
   a wicked little goblin
   from a dark and dreary wood.

I'll wear a face, a frightful face
   from the Five-and-Ten-Cent Store,
   and frighten Mrs. Brady
   who lives alone next door.

I'll frighten everyone who lives
   on our side of the street—
   even the big policeman,
   and everyone I meet.

The Ghost

Just as the day goes into night,
    when all downstairs is lighted bright,
    and I climb into Daddy's chair
    to read him make-up stories there—
    I think it's mean as mean can be
    when I'm not sleepy after tea
    and only half a story's read,
    for them to march me up to bed.

The room's too dark—and I don't dare
    to look into that corner there.
    It's Mother's shawl upon the hook,
    I know—but I don't dare to look.

If I were more than half past five,
    I'd be the bravest boy alive.
    I'd throw the covers off my head,
    sit up as straight and strong in bed,
    look right into that corner square,
    and call quite loud, "Who's there? Who's there?"

It's Mother's shawl—I'm sure—almost—
    but still it looks just like a ghost—
    the very one 'bout which I read
    before they marched me up to bed!

I'm not afraid—but still—I think
    I'll call and ask them for a drink.

The Roller Skater

Away
away
   up Shady Street
   where sky and pavement seem to meet
   and the old church bell in the steeple tall
   calls out to me,
   "Take care! Don't fall!"—
   I like to start from our front gate
   and skate and skate and skate and skate
   until I reach the very top
   and then roll down without a stop!

When I was three, last year, you know,
   I really was afraid to go
   up Shady Street and round the square
   because a great white goat lived there—
   with a long white beard and horns that curled,
   the biggest goat in all the world!
   But now I skate so swiftly by,
   he could not catch me if he'd try.

Sometimes I am a ship at sea
   with all the breezes blowing me—
   sometimes a fish, I'm swimming by—
   sometimes a bird, I dip and fly
   away
   away
   up Shady Street
   where sky and pavement seem to meet
   and the old church bell in the steeple tall
   calls out to me, "Take care! Don't fall!"

All Day Across the River

All day across the river
   from Irondale I see
   the beautiful Kentucky hills
   behaving beautif'ly.

Sometimes they look so green and glad
   they call to me and say,
   "Come over! Ask your mother
   to let you come and play!"

My mother says Kentucky hills
   are loveliest of all
   when leaping into sunset
   as the dark begins to fall.

They're black and beautiful and sad
   above the golden river
   when one white star breaks through the blue
   and the moon's a silver sliver.

Sometimes they are so beautiful
   they make my mother cry—
   at twilight when their edges
   cut sharp into the sky.

The Man in the Moon

When the day is gone
   and the dark comes on
      and the sky is a blue, blue sea,
the man in the moon
   comes sailing soon
      and stares and stares at me.

All round and still
   from behind the hill
      where he smells the wild flowers growing,
he comes sailing bright
   up the purple night
      with the silvery clouds a-blowing.

And all the while
   he does not smile
      at me, or care for joking,
for he does not know
   when the soft winds blow
      that he looks as though he's smoking!

He does not wink;
   he does not blink
      as he stares and stares at me,
when the day is gone
   and the dark comes on
      and the sky is a blue, blue sea.

Promoted

That girl—Rosemary Miller—she
   sits just across the aisle from me.
   Her cheeks are very round and red,
   and on the tiptop of her head
   all bobbed off short and straight and brown—
   she wears the biggest bow in town.
   When she drinks from her silver cup
   she doesn't raise her lashes up.

They say she's only half past five
   and she's the smartest girl alive!
   She knows her numbers up to ten,
   can write her name, "dog," "cat" and "hen,"
   can speak two pieces, start the song
   and lead the march and not go wrong!
   She freckles even when it's shady,
   and tries to walk just like a lady.

They say her mother calls her "Roses,"
   and spoils her so that she supposes
   that even boys have got to do
   exactly as she wants them to!
   She's mad at me and doesn't speak,
   because I called her "Apple-cheek."
   She holds her head up in the air
   as though she thinks that I'm not there;

But when the teacher read the list
   of those that passed and those that missed,
   that girl—Rosemary Miller—she
   turned round and smiled and smiled at me

and sat up proud enough to burst—
for she's promoted to High First
and got the only card with pink
"Distinction" written in red ink.

Last Night

Last night when I was lying
   in bed by the window sill
   a fat old moon came spying
   behind old Sunrise Hill.

A jolly moon all orange red
   and bulging big as three—
   I drew the sheet above my head
   to keep him from spying me.

I peeped at him and dared him
   to find me where I lay,
   but a little dog barked and scared him
   and he turned pale and gray.

A baby bird in the sycamore
   began to fret and cry;
   a sparrow laughed from the big barn door,
   and a star ran down the sky.

At the Window

Star—star—shining bright—
    what holds you up there in the night?
    Aren't you afraid of falling?
    Can you see me? Hear me calling?

Do star-children run and play
    up and down the Milky Way?
    Do you ever long to be
    just a little child like me?

Are you cold? What makes you shiver
    as you shine above the river?
    Star—star—shining bright—
    what holds you up there in the night?

Our Flag

Red as the rose
   white as the snows
      blue as the sky
         it floats and blows.

Floats and blows
  for you and me
     over the land
        over the sea!

The Exile

I'm up and dressed—but have to stay
   in this same room another day.

The night I wakened sick-abed
   with all that fever in my head,
   the roses on the bedroom walls
   turned into laughing dancing dolls!
   The old clock sniffed and stared at me,
   surprised and shocked as it could be
   to see my quiet old bed posts
   turn into ogres, goblins, ghosts,
   that scampered off into their lair
   when they heard Mother on the stair.

But now they don't come out and play—
   the roses stay the same old way;
   the bed posts stand as still and grave
   as though they could not misbehave;
   the old clock on the mantel wall
   just ticks and ticks and strikes—that's all.

I'm up and dressed—but have to stay
   in this same room another day
   because it had to go and rain.

That wet wasp on the window pane
   would rather be a wasp and free
   than any boy shut in like me.

The Swimmers

I see them—oh, I see them
   every summer afternoon
   when the world is hot and shiny
   after school is out in June—
   Johnny Jones and Jimmy Johnson
   and a lot of boys I know
   all a-hurrying down to the river
   as fast as they can go—
   and I have to ride with mother
   in the back seat of the car
   and see them all go swimming
   down the road at Sandy Bar!

They never have to dress in white
   with sandals on and socks—
   they hide their shirts and trousers
   anywhere among the rocks—
   they don't take any bathing suits
   or towels or toilet soap;
   they haven't any water wings;
   there isn't any rope—
   they swim and dive all afternoon
   or play they're Indian braves
   or pirates after treasure
   in the gloomy river caves,
   and never start for home until
   the dark begins to grow
   and the sun hangs like a lantern
   down the river bend below.

And when in time for supper
they all go slipping in,
their fathers and their mothers
never ask them where they've been.

Nap Time

Some day
some day
  some day instead of sleeping—
  with all the world so full of things to do—
  I'll softly slip away, my secret keeping
  from everyone but God, dear doll, and you—
  I'll climb the hill,
  the green hill over yonder,
  that looks a lovely ladder to the sky,
  and play awhile with silvery clouds that wander
  with their mothers in the meadows of the sky—
  for I want to touch the blue,
  to see if it is true
  that the hill's a lovely ladder to the sky.

Some night
some night
  some night instead of sleeping,
  with all the world so cool and wet with dew,
  I'll softly slip away, my secret keeping,
  from everyone but God, dear doll, and you—
  I'll climb the hill,
  the green hill over yonder,
  that looks a lovely ladder to the sky,
  and play awhile with silvery stars that wander
  with their mother-moon in meadows blue and high—
  for I want to touch the blue,
  to see if it is true
  that the hill's a lovely ladder to the sky.

Once—

Down in the garden of my heart,
  a child once played a wondrous part.
It was morn. Over the hills her flying feet
led me on to the lure of her laughter sweet
and a sad-glad look; ah, my hour was fleet!
For she turned on a path I do not know
and has left me alone in the afterglow.
It is night. O'er the hills the sun is set,
and her sad-glad face with the soft lips wet
is gone—though her love is with me yet.

Summers may come and summers go,
  a myriad roses bloom and blow,
  a myriad roseal worlds may run
  in rapture round a mother-sun—
  and all were mockery—every one—
  unless the child that came to play
  in my heart's garden for a day
  be mine again; unless somewhere,
  in some serene, diviner air,
  she waits—until I find her there.

V

I Must Have Thirsted

I must have thirsted
  for a thousand years
  to win the slaking rapture
  of your tears—

I must have bared me
  to a thousand swords
  to win the naked lightning
  of your words—

I must have conquered
  hells that seethe and hiss
  to win the sudden heaven
  of your kiss—

A Look—A Light

A look, a light
   between two prison towers,
   a breath of woods, wet earth
   and sudden showers—

A lovely, lonely light
   invades the sky—
   so sharp a joy
   can joy itself defy—
   but, stranger, live;
   let me be first to die.

I Burn a Secret Candle

I burn a secret candle
   for none but you to see—
   the want of you,
   the haunt of you,
   the dear withholding taunt of you
   to teach me poverty,

And though I go a beggar
   hugging a darling pain,
   the truth of you,
   the ruth of you,
   the deep undying youth of you
   of whom I dream in vain,

Not all the midnight censers
   of suns and worlds in line
   can swing to you
   or sing to you
   or madly, gladly fling to you
   as rich a gift as mine.

I Flung a Rose

I flung a rose to you,
  my one red rose;
  swiftly I flung it, eager, reckless, blind—
  my life's red rose—
  you caught and kissed it
  and were only kind.

You might have trampled it,
  my one red rose,
  blessed it with death, as men humanely kill—
  a foolish, hapless thing,
  my life's red rose—
  you might have crushed it
  and been kinder still.

Sometimes in Dreams

Sometimes in dreams a simple thing
   can make a muted spirit sing.

I had a dream surpassing sweet—
   I met you in a crowded street
   and walked with you a little way
   as many indifferent others may.

You smiled and showed a glad surprise,
   held me a moment in your eyes—
   a moment exquisite and new
   from deeps where only dreams speak true,

And suddenly the city lane
   went fresh as lilacs drenched with rain,
   and Pan with all his crazy crew
   came dancing there for me and you.

Sometimes in dreams a simple thing
   can make a muted spirit sing
   and lift a singing fool like me
   to lilac time in Arcady.

Jealousy

The wily winds come whispering
   across the world to me,
     "She's young and sweet and tender
   and beautiful to see."

They rattle at my window
   the bones of deviltry;
     "Spring-sweet and lithe and slender
   as a young birch tree."

"Begone," I cry, "he loves me."
   They laugh derisively;
     "A young birch in the moonlight
   is a lovely thing to see."

You Are So Cold

You are so cold, so silent, so untender—
   as water to your star
   you hold me as a mirror for your splendor
   from very high and far.

My woodland pool, my sea, my river gropings
   cannot encompass you
   who bathe your beauty in my hopeless hopings,
   as stars, perchance, may do.

White Blooms

White blooms you give to me,
   cool buds packed tight,
   and never a bud uncloses—
   cool buds, dead white,
   that never come to roses.

Believe in Me

Believe in me—though with a rod
   to flay me out of rest;
   scourge me with your faith and rouse the god
   in me to meet your test—

Believe in me—though with a spark
   from very high and far,
   and all my rich and silent dark
   may blaze into a star.

Believe in me and love me too,
   although from far and high;
   I'm mute at what I'd dream and do
   and dare before I die.

Like a Comet

Sir, like a comet doomed to run
   through mocking centuries toward the sun,
   constrained by time and tide and space
  to seek forever your embrace,
  I ran to you. And niggard fate,
  foreknowing I was wrong and late,
  looked on and laughed. All I could do
  was blow a burning kiss to you,
  who, sated with the eternal play,
  would scarcely deign to look my way—
  without a word of love to say.

Your Silence Is Like God's

Your silence is like God's
  and that of every god
    since life began the spawn of man.

Your silence beggars death
  for simple cruelty,
    and yet it speaks the things you do not say.

All Cool and Blue

All cool and blue the shadows fall;
   The twilight star is white and high;
I hear the vesper-sparrow call,
   Sweetheart! I love you—love you—love you—
   And night is nigh.

Ah, sweetheart, I who walk alone
   Through evening beauty, like a nun,
I would my heart against your own
   Could cry, I love you—love you—love you—
   When day is done.

Fiesole

Where Arno's gently swelling breast
   nipples to many a mountain crest—
   in one immortal hour of play,
   on one wild windfall of a day,
   I drank pure beauty on the way
   from Florence to Fiesole.

Fiesole—
Fiesole—
   a sunlit sapphire word to say—
   to say it is to sing a lay
   of lovelinesses white and high
   against a blue-black deep of sky
   with dials of darkling cypress towers
   to show forth the slender hours
   fainting beneath the blaze of noon,
   rising to meet a midnight moon.

Beguiled into a cypress glade
   I stretched me on a bed of shade
   and from the deep blue bowl of sky
   I drank—for still my throat was dry—
   of pagan steams that dared to flow
   from a forbidden long ago.

While through my quickening nostrils ran
   the earthy ecstasy of Pan,
   fresh as a rainy petal spray
   of April on the mouth of May,
   in beauty, like a mountain troll,
   I dared to saturate my soul.

Through veils of centuries withdrawn
  I looked into another dawn—
  saw nymphs come dancing unafraid
  with frail young fauns on hoofs of jade,
  amazed, alert, arrested, shy
  at sight of such a one as I.

Beloved, did I dream or see
  a faun like you, a nymph like me
  in that immortal hour of play
  on mountaintop Fiesole?

And so if men shall call me fey,
  down in the streets of every day,
  be wise who will and mock who may;
  for one immortal draught of wine
  who would not drink and pay the fine?
  I've had a priceless hour of play
  on mountaintop Fiesole.

Fiesole—
Fiesole—
  a singing, sighing word to say—
  to say it is to sing a lay
  of some soft, sunny yesterday—
  I know not where, I know not why
  to say it is to sing a sigh
  for lovelinesses long gone by—
  for beauty born to breathe and die.

VI

Europe—1914

I saw a thousand towers—cathedral towers—
   arise serene and white
   into the blue of crystal morning hours,
   into the silvery night—

I heard them sing above the human clan
   at work and play and learning
   a song of love, of brotherhood for man,
   of life beyond death's turning—

When, lo, the souls that sent the lily towers
   aspiring to the sky,
   reminding men at dawn and sunset hours
   of love that must not die—

I saw them rushing passionate for gain,
   storming a brother's gate,
   blasting his temples, making all the plain
   a slaughter pit for hate!

* * *

Not yet, O lowly, lovely Nazarene,
   your temple towers arise—

not yet while such a human scene
can dawn on children's eyes.

Two thousand years—and still the hell of war
to meet at any turn,
two thousand years since Christ. How many more,
O man, until you learn?

Noël

Even angels
   can but grieve
   at sight of earth
   on Christmas Eve—

One frightened child,
   bereft, forlorn,
   should darken heaven
   on Christmas morn—

Unnumbered children,
   bombed, aflame,
   should set a universe
   to shame.

Many years since Jesus came
   to Bethlehem and brought it fame—
   the genius of a tale sublime
   who conquered death and space and time—
   whose star lights every year anew—
   that child, that Jesus, was a Jew.

Christmas Wine—1940

What sort of comfort shall we take,
  we who have wine and bread,
  while war has left a widening wake
  of lives undone, unfed?

What sort of loving cup shall slake
  our throats with Christmas wine,
  while multitudes have shock and quake
  and death on which to dine?

What sort of joy shall dull the ache
  for youth whose hope is laid,
  for babes that lisp "for Jesus' sake,"
  frightened, forlorn, betrayed?

What sort of prayer shall we make
  beside an easy bed,
  with human freedom now at stake,
  truth crushed and beauty dead?

May Was Not May—1917

May was not May—June is not June,
    though the plum tree is white at the door—
    it seems to me white as the bride of a night,
    whose lover went off to the war.

The robins are calling their loves from the trees;
    the roses are red on the walls—
    they seem to me red as the blood of the dead
    on the breast of a youth when he falls.

His father is rich, his mother is kind,
    and the house stands so grand on the hill—
    but early and late every room seems to wait
    for a voice and a step that is still.

Target—Berlin, 1918

Target tonight, Berlin—when you and I
   conspire to shower destruction from the sky;
   we who love gardens, houses, children, dogs,
   school bells and church bells, Christmas greens and logs;
   we who tonight put precious babes to sleep,
   imploring heaven their tender lives to keep.

Berlin, your crimes that count a bloody host
   are one—the crime against the human ghost
   that puts on decent souls the shock and shame
   of dealing desolation in life's name.

Christmas 1939

The Christmas towers ring out again
   a song of peace, good will to men;
   a million hearts unite to sing
   the story of a newborn King—
   the Child who in a manger lay
   warm in the soft, sweet lap of hay,
   a mother's face above Him bending
   with shepherds from the hills attending—
   still staggered at the sound and sight
   of angels singing in the night,
   while over Bethlehem's peaceful sky
   a stranger star burned white and high,
   announcing to the wayward earth
   the moment of the Saviour's birth.

Afar—the singing towers are crushed,
   the Christmas caroling is hushed;
   the Christmas snow is spattered red,
   the singing youths are lying dead;
   again the earth is gashed with trenches,
   the air is thick with gassy stenches;
   along the roads, bewildered, flying,
   mothers and children wailing, crying.

How long, O loving Nazarene,
   shall madmen make the human scene
   a shambles—in a maniac game
   that puts the earth and man to shame?

Hitler

What smirking smith
   has hammered into flame
   the spark
   the glare
   the madness
   of this name?

What cosmic captain
   summons us to help
   against this shriek
   this fury
   and this yelp?

What fate decrees
   the decent human clan
   take up again
   the club of Caliban?

America, 1942

Lay down the lute, the brush, the pen—
   the beast and beauty fight again.

Since fight we must for freedom's sake,
   the joy of life itself at stake—
   take up the sword—plunge deep and red
   until the attacking beast is dead.

For what would human breath be worth,
 with freedom banished from the earth,
 truth crucified, and beauty mute
 beneath the trampling of the brute?

Take up the sword—plunge deep and red
 until the attacking brute is dead.

Children Evacuated From London, 1943

Let us live, work, fight and pray
 for the coming Christmas Day
 when each newborn babe of earth
 shall know freedom from its birth.

Let us hang above this night
 such a star of love and light
 every child shall wake to find
 earth a joying place and kind,

Where he may serve fearlessly
 his creative destiny,
 venture, suffer, learn, laugh, sing—
 add to life some precious thing.

Gandhi

Let Gandhi die—
   let Gandhi die—

   they whispered when
   the end was nigh—

   three lethal words
   outside his tent
   to end his patient argument—

   and though
   no miracle at dawn
   left bare the mat he died upon,

   removed the rack of skin and bone
   to prove that life had claimed its own,

   writ red across the sky we see
   another deathless Calvary.

The Murderer (1915)

May 19   Arrived at the penitentiary today.
              I must exist in the death annex for four months.
              Why do I have to live so long?

May 22   A letter from Mother in far-off Warsaw.
                 Father Limke wrote it.

              Hope to God she never hears of my predicament!
              She has suffered enough—from my temper—and from
                 my father's.

              I am to be punished—with death.
              Who will make it up to her?

May 23   Sunday.

              They marched me to the chapel.
              I could not sing or pray. I could only think.

              I asked the guard to show me the electric chair.
              He would not. I wonder why?

May 25   Outside, the newsboys shout about the war in Europe.
              Within—I sit in a grave.

              If I could only give my life for Poland!

              Europe is a slaughter pit. Belgium and Poland are
                 innocent.
              I am not that kind of murderer. Strunksky was guilty.

             The judge knew that Strunksky was not fit to live.
             Why am I punished so severely?

May 30   Memorial Day.
             The bands play.
             The veterans march with the children.
             They place flowers on beloved graves.
             The wind breathes through the flowers. Outside it is all
                fragrance, music, color.

             Next year, where I lie, no one will lay flowers.
             But a child might stray there.

             Does one who kills in sudden rage have a heart as black
                as one who steals from childhood?

June 3   It rains. Little rivers run in the yard.
             Outside it is cool and fresh.

             My eyes burn dry—my hands—my feet—my head.
             I would like to lie cool and dead at the bottom of a river.
             I would like to lie on a hilltop—dead—with the rain
                on my face.

             Three months from today I die.

             Death is as good as birth, even if there be purgatory.
             Life in the stockyards was hell.

             Will I falter when the black cap is drawn over my head?
             Will I fight with my last strength for my life?
             I was always a fighter.

To turn the death-switch on a man—that also is murder.
I could not do that. I am not that kind of murderer.

June 9   The Russians are pressing the Germans back—the guard tells me.

Can Warsaw be in danger?

Poor Mother! Poor Poland! To suffer for others' sins.

June 12   Saturday. Pay day once, with supper at the dancehall with Natascha.

I had not thought I could write her name!

With whom does she dance now? For she dances.

Not with me—or Strunksky!

He was clumsy on his feet. I struck him only once.
I could not know his head would hit the curb.
How could I? He might have lived.

Then I would have gone free.

Is death painless?
What is the great beyond?

June 20   Another Sunday.

In chapel they told me that Bill and Joe go free tomorrow.

They will see Natascha.
I sent her no word. What does she care?

Women are the cause of all the trouble in the world.
I gave her my heart and my money.
She gave me back my heart and kept the money.

June 27 These Sundays will drive me mad!

Does God need to be persuaded by men? Does he like to be praised?

We do not choose to come into the world. We have to struggle, suffer, blunder.

Poland was hell. In Chicago the stockyards were hell.
All I had was Natascha.

The Kaiser thanks God for victorious murder. He thinks God is pleased.
I am not that kind of murderer. I do not believe that of God.
God is greater than all of this.

July 4 I am in the hospital!
I may die before September—before the day of the death chair!
They tell me it is quick consumption.
If only it be quick enough!

Jimmy Doyle—in the next bed—is happy today.
His sentence is reduced to life imprisonment.
He is only twenty.

I am thirty-three. Too young to die. Too worn out to live.

August 29   Still in the hospital.
A paper came from the judge. Father Sobieski translated it into Polish.
I am not to die on Friday! I am to live until December. It is a postponement.

The death chair for my Christmas gift!

The priest brought me an orange.
In Poland, one Christmas, my mother brought me an orange from the great house. I was a very little boy. She told me of the birthday of Jesus.

Jesus was murdered.
I shall go quickly. They murdered Jesus slowly— on a cross.

Now they who build cathedrals in his name
Blast the cathedrals and murder each other.
They want territory, riches, power.
I am not that kind of a murderer.

I wanted only to marry Natascha—to work for her.
I hoped that we would have children.
I thought, some day, to send for Mother.